Triassic Period
203 – 196 million years ago
Carnivore

Coelophysis

This book belongs to:

Dueling Dinosaurs &
Prehistoric Beasts
Carnivores & Herbivores

Coloring Book,
Connect the Dots,
& Fun Facts!

Mary Lou Brown & Sandy Mahony

Carnivores eat meat or fish.

Herbivores eat plants.

Dimetrodon

Carnivore

Early Permian Period, 295-272 million years ago

Dimetrodon is not a dinosaur. It became extinct 40 million years before dinosaurs. It is considered a mammal-like-reptile. Dimetrodon, a predator, fed on fish, reptiles, and amphibians.

Plesiosaur
Carnivore

Late Triassic, Jurassic, & Cretaceous Periods, 203.6-66 million years ago

Plesiosaurs swam in all oceans of the world. They breathed air and ate fish and other sea animals. Some had long necks, and small heads, and others had short necks and large heads.

Stegosaurus

Herbivore

Late Jurassic Period, 155-150 million years ago

Stegosaurus had a double row of plates (17-22) on its rounded back. It lived in herds and fed on low-lying bushes or shrubs, including ferns, mosses, conifers, or fruit. Allosaurus may have been one of its predators.

Allosaurus

Carnivore

Late Jurassic Period, 155-150 million years ago

Allosaurus was a large predator that fed on large herbivore dinosaurs and possibly other carnivores. It had a huge skull with dozens of sharp teeth, two small front limbs, two large back limbs, and a muscular tail.

Apatosaurus

Herbivore

Late Jurassic Period, 155-152 million years ago

Apatosaurus is a giant, long-necked dinosaur with a small head, a square snout, and teeth suited for eating plants. Its whip-like tail is capable of creating loud noises. It is sometimes called a Brontosaurus.

Pterodactyl

Carnivore

Late Jurassic Period, 150.8-148.5 million years ago

Pterodactyls, flying reptiles, were carnivores that ate fish and other small animals. Its wings stretched from its fourth finger to its hind legs with an estimated span of over three feet.

Baryonyx

Carnivore

Early Cretaceous Period, 130-125 million years ago

Baryonyx means "heavy claw" and refers to its enormous first-finger claw. It ate fish and lived near bodies of water. It may also have been a predator of larger prey and a scavenger.

Spinosaurus

Carnivore

Cretaceous Period, 112-97 million years ago

Spinosaurus is one of the longest and largest carnivorous dinosaurs. It could be as long as 49-59 feet. Its skull is long and narrow, similar to a crocodile. It lived on land and in water and ate fish and land prey.

Corythosaurus

Herbivore

Cretaceous Period, 77-75.7 million years ago

Corythosaurus means "helmet lizard" and had a short skull with a high helmet-like crest. The structure of the crest made it possible for Corythosaurus to make loud, trombone-sounding warning calls.

Parasaurolophus

Herbivore

Late Cretaceous Period, 76.5-74.5 million years ago

The rare Parasaurolophus had an elaborate crest on its head, which formed a long curved tube projecting upward and back from the skull. It was able to walk on either two or four legs.

Styracosaurus

Herbivore

Cretaceous Period, 75.5-75 million years ago

Styracosaurus, "spike lizard," had four to six long horns on its neck, a smaller horn on each cheek, a large horn on its nose, and a beak-like mouth. With a bulky body and short legs, it resembled a rhinoceros.

Velociraptor

Carnivore

Cretaceous Period, 75-71 million years ago

Velociraptor, "swift seizer," walked on two legs and had a large claw on each hind foot. The claw was used to tear into or capture prey. It has been characterized as a flightless bird and probably had feathers.

Triceratops
Herbivore

Late Cretaceous Period, 68-66 million years ago

Triceratops, "three-horned-face," has three facial horns and a bony frill on its neck. It became extinct, along with three-quarters of the plant and animal species on Earth, during the Cretaceous-Paleogene extinction event triggered by effects on the environment from a huge comet impact.

Tyrannosaurus

Carnivore

Late Cretaceous Period, 68-66 million years ago

Tyrannosaurus, "tyrant lizard," is among the largest land predators with a massive skull, long, heavy tail, and powerful hind legs. Known as a fierce predator, it was also a scavenger.

Ankylosaurus
Herbivore

Late Cretaceous Period, 68-66 million years ago

A striking feature of Ankylosaurus was its armor, consisting of knobs and plates of bone embedded in the skin. They may have been slow moving animals, but likely capable of quick movements if necessary.

Mammoth

Herbivore

Pliocene, Pleistocene, and Holocene epochs, 5 million - 4,500 years ago

Close relatives of modern elephants, mammoths had long, curved tusks and in the northern regions, were covered with long hair. Extinction may have been caused by glacial retreat, rising sea waters, and the spread of human hunters.

Smilodon
Saber-toothed Cat

Carnivore

Pleistocene epoch, 2.5 million - 10,000 years ago

Commonly known as the saber-toothed tiger, it was not closely related to the tiger. Smilodon hunted large herbivores such as bison and camels. It lived in forests and bush, which provided cover for hunting prey.

Mastodon

Herbivore

Pleistocene epoch, 10,000 ~ 11,000 years ago

Mastodons are distant relatives to mammoths and modern elephants. They lived in herds and were forest dwelling animals, eating twigs and browsing on trees and shrubs. Hunting by humans may have led to extinction.

16

17

15

18

20

27

28

25   26   29

24   30

31

14   19

13   12   21   22   23   32

11   5   33

9   6   3   34

10   7   4   2

8   1

Pterodactyl

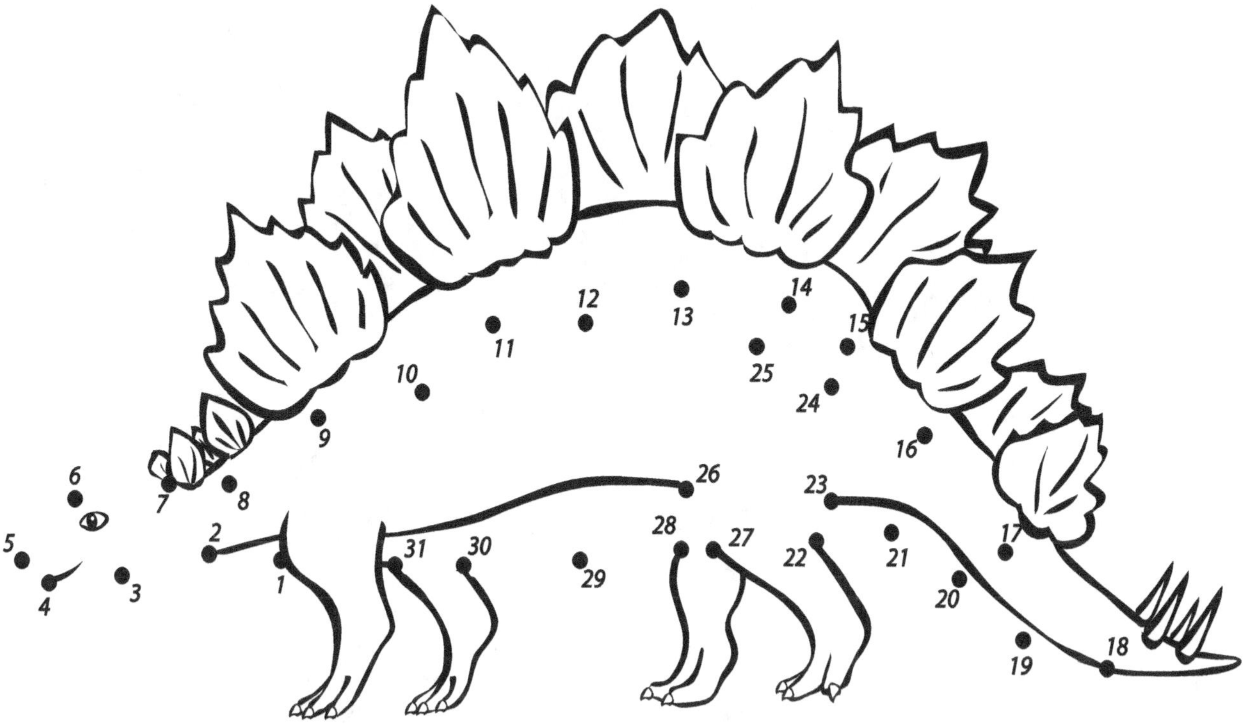

Stegosaurus

Tyrannosaur

Triceratops

Smilodon

Spinosaurus

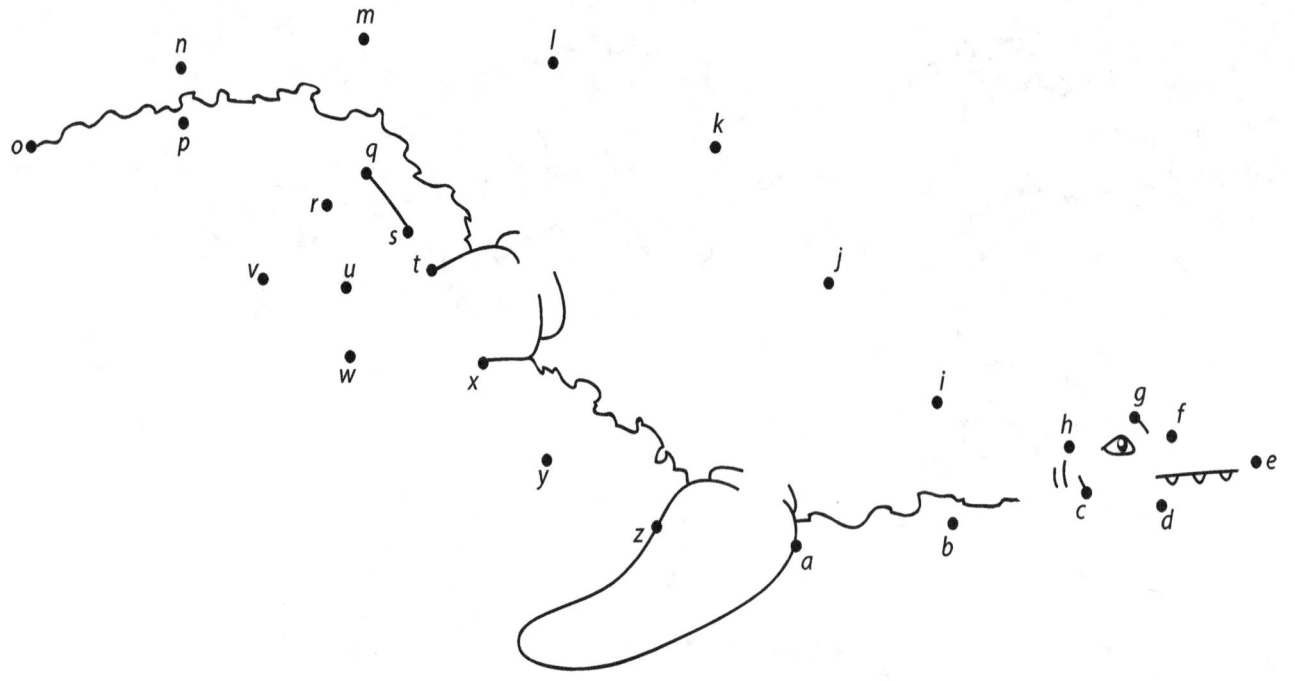

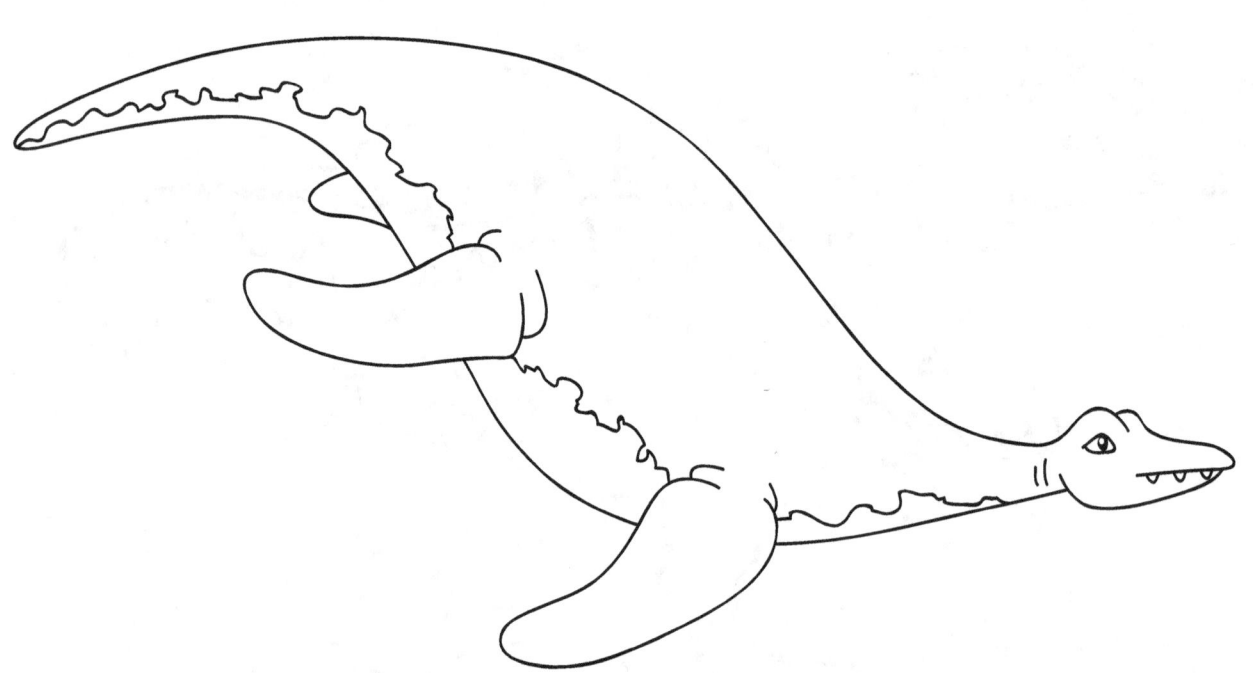

Plesiosaur

Parasaurolophus

Styracosaurus

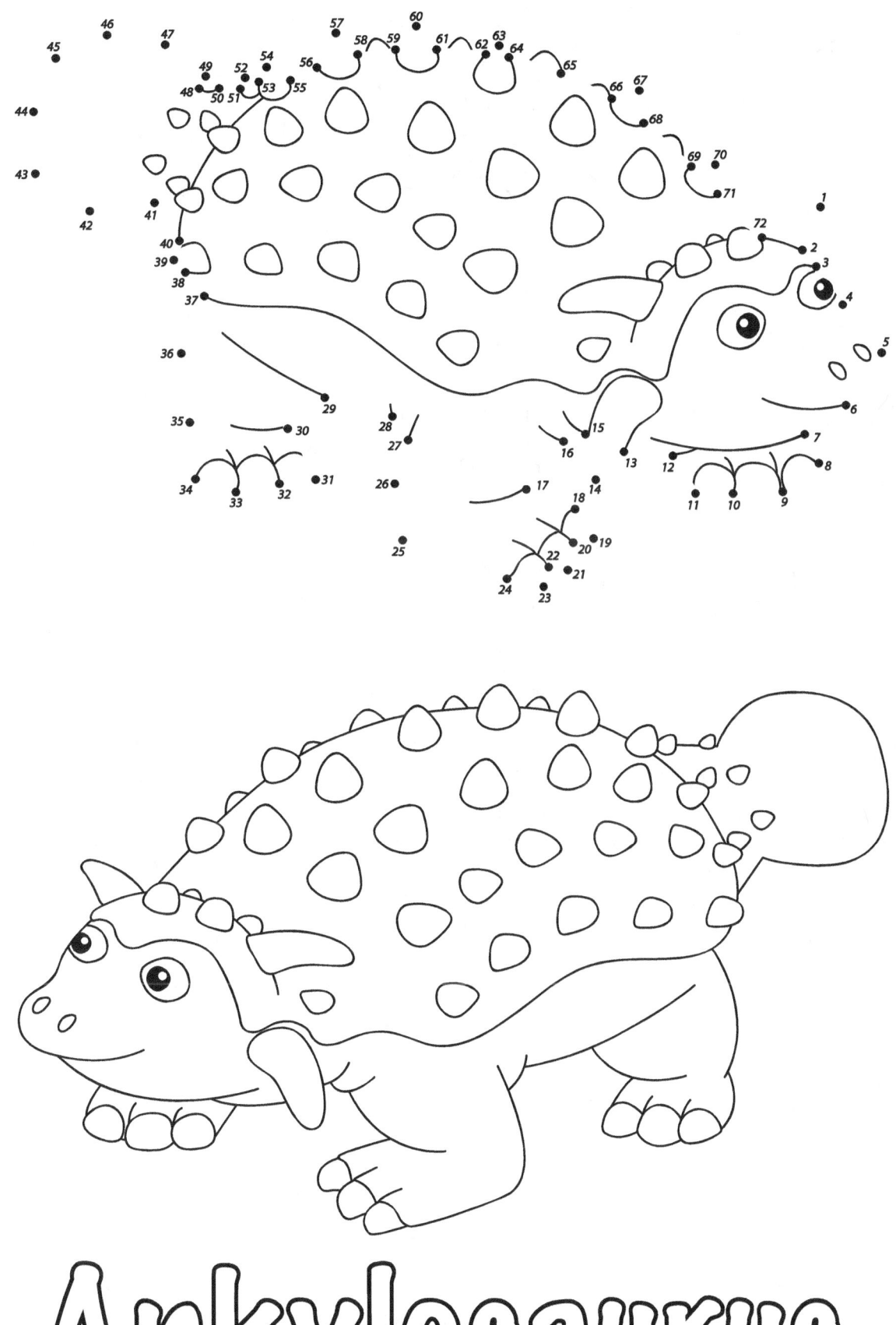

Ankylosaurus

adventurelearningpress.com

Adventure
Learning
Press